HOLY**HABITS** BIBLE REFLECTIONS | BREAKING BREAD

The Bible Reading Fellowship
15 The Chambers, Vineyard
Abingdon OX14 3FE
brf.org.uk

The Bible Reading Fellowship (BRF) is a Registered Charity (233280)

ISBN 978 0 85746 838 3
First published 2020
10 9 8 7 6 5 4 3 2 1 0
All rights reserved

Text © individual authors 2020
This edition © The Bible Reading Fellowship 2020
Original design by morsebrowndesign.co.uk & penguinboy.net

The authors assert the moral right to be identified as the authors
of this work

Acknowledgements

Scripture quotations marked NRSV are taken from The New Revised
Standard Version of the Bible, Anglicised edition, copyright © 1989, 1995
by the Division of Christian Education of the National Council of the
Churches of Christ in the United States of America. Used by permission.
All rights reserved.

Scripture quotations marked NIV are taken from The Holy Bible, New
International Version (Anglicised edition) copyright © 1979, 1984, 2011
by Biblica. Used by permission of Hodder & Stoughton Publishers, a
Hachette UK company. All rights reserved. 'NIV' is a registered trademark
of Biblica. UK trademark number 1448790.

Every effort has been made to trace and contact copyright owners
for material used in this resource. We apologise for any inadvertent
omissions or errors, and would ask those concerned to contact us so that
full acknowledgement can be made in the future.

A catalogue record for this book is available from the British Library

Printed and bound in the UK by Zenith Media NP4 0DQ

BREAKING BREAD

BIBLE REFLECTIONS
40 READINGS AND REFLECTIONS

Edited by
ANDREW ROBERTS

Contents

Contents

Contents

About the writers

Rob Glenny is rector of the Radley, Sunningwell and Kennington benefice, situated between Oxford and Abingdon. Prior to ordination he read for degrees in theology at the universities of St Andrews and Oxford.

Derek Tidball was formerly the principal of London School of Theology. He is a prolific writer and a speaker in demand around the world. He is the New Testament editor for BRF's 'Really Useful Guides' series.

Naomi Starkey is a curate in the Church in Wales, working in Welsh and English across six rural churches on the Llyn Peninsula. She previously worked as a BRF commissioning editor from 1997 to 2015 and has written a number of books, including *The Recovery of Joy* (BRF, 2017) and *The Recovery of Hope* (BRF, 2016).

Liz Kent is director of Wesley Study Centre, Durham University, and minister for Chester le Street, Birtley and Pelton Methodist Churches. She studied law at Liverpool University prior to training for Methodist ministry. She is interested in questions of holiness, Christian ethics and mission, and completed PhD research at Durham University exploring the church and eating disorders. She is a keen drummer, footballer and outdoor pursuits enthusiast. She is married to Ian, also a Methodist minister, and they have two daughters.

Introduction to Holy Habits

> They devoted themselves to the apostles' teaching and fellowship, to the breaking of bread and the prayers. Awe came upon everyone, because many wonders and signs were being done by the apostles. All who believed were together and had all things in common; they would sell their possessions and goods and distribute the proceeds to all, as any had need. Day by day, as they spent much time together in the temple, they broke bread at home and ate their food with glad and generous hearts, praising God and having the goodwill of all the people. And day by day the Lord added to their number those who were being saved.
>
> ACTS 2:42–47 (NRSV)

Holy Habits is a way of forming disciples that is emerging anew from an exploration of this precious portion of scripture, Luke's famous portrait of the early church. As such, it is both deeply biblical and an approach that lives when infused with the life-giving breath of the Holy Spirit – the same Holy Spirit who brought life, energy and creativity to the first Christian communities.

Holy Habits is based upon a series of ten practices that are shown to be fruitful in the Acts 2 passage: biblical teaching, fellowship, breaking bread, prayer, sharing resources, serving, eating together, gladness and generosity, worship, and making more disciples. In this series of material, passages relating to the ten habits are explored one habit at a time, sometimes with reference to other habits. In real life, the habits all get mixed up and complement each other as part of a holistic way of discipleship. You may want to be alert to such connections.

There are many lists in the Bible, and with biblical lists the first and last items often have particular significance. In this list, it is significant that biblical teaching comes first. All of the habits are to be found throughout scripture, and healthy holy habits will be grounded in regular engagement with biblical teaching. This is a foundational habit.

The last habit is also significant. Commentators have remarked that it is no surprise that 'day by day the Lord added to their number' when life was lived in the way Luke describes. Many can be nervous of the word 'evangelism'. Holy Habits offers a way of being evangelistic that may help to assuage some of those nerves.

Holy Habits is a way of life for followers of Jesus individually and collectively. In Acts 2:42–47, Luke offers clues as to how these practices can be fruitful. Note the devotion he mentions at the beginning and the repeated use of the word 'all'. Holy Habits is a way of life for all ages (including children), cultures and contexts. The habits are to be lived day by day, in the whole of life, Monday to Saturday as well as Sunday. And note how Luke attributes the growth that results to the Lord. These are *holy* habits, which flourish when the Lord is at the centre of all.

Introduction to Breaking Bread

Breaking bread is the only one of the holy habits that Luke mentions twice in Acts 2:42–47. Clearly it was a significant part of the devotional and missional life of the earliest Christian communities. Intriguingly, in the first reference in verse 42, in the original Greek Luke speaks of the breaking of *the* bread. The inclusion of the definite article, not used in most English translations, suggests this could signify bread being broken as part of an early organised form of Holy Communion. But then on the second occasion Luke says, 'They broke bread at home and ate their food' – suggesting that bread may have been broken by the believers as part of their eating together. This was common practice in Jewish households of the time, but would have had new meaning and significance for those who were now followers of Jesus.

The biblical commentator Hans Conzelmann points out that Luke makes no attempt to distinguish between an ordinary meal and the Eucharist and suggests that 'the unity of the two is part of the ideal picture of the earliest church' (*The Acts of the Apostles*, Fortress, 1987, p. 23). The unity of the two is seen particularly powerfully in the eucharistic meal that Paul shares with his fellow sailors in Acts 27:35. Their meal on the ship begins with Paul giving thanks and breaking bread. Encouraged and renewed spiritually, they are then nourished and strengthened physically as they eat together.

In the book *Holy Habits* (Andrew Roberts, Malcolm Down Publishing, 2016) and the church resource booklets (published by BRF in 2018), these two ways of seeing and practising breaking bread are noted and *both* are encouraged. That encouragement is also present in these Bible reflections. Here, the writers reflect upon a range of texts from the Hebrew scriptures and the New Testament in which bread features. Rob and Liz apply insights from the texts that they engage with to a range of contexts in which bread is broken and shared. Derek focuses more on bread in the context of eating together, while Naomi gives particular attention to breaking bread in the context of the Eucharist.

When it comes to breaking bread in the gathered worship of the church, different Christians have different titles for the act that Jesus said we are to do in memory of him: the Eucharist, Holy Communion and the Lord's Supper are just some of them. In these notes, each writer uses their own preferred term. If/when this varies from your preferred term, you may wish to notice what can be learnt from the usage of other terms.

One final thought: in a conversation about breaking bread, one prominent Christian leader asked, 'Why have we made something Jesus deliberately made so simple and transferable, so complicated?' It is a good question. As you read and pray though these reflections, you may wish to be alert to simple ways in which you can break bread wherever you are, both as an act of thanksgiving and as a way of making Jesus known.

The power of bread and wine

Genesis 14:17–20

After his return from the defeat of Chedorlaomer and the kings who were with him, the king of Sodom went out to meet him at the Valley of Shaveh (that is, the King's Valley). And King Melchizedek of Salem brought out bread and wine; he was priest of God Most High. He blessed him and said, 'Blessed be Abram by God Most High, maker of heaven and earth; and blessed be God Most High, who has delivered your enemies into your hand!' And Abram gave him one-tenth of everything.   (NRSV)

| Rob Glenny

Reflection

There are striking eucharistic overtones in the actions of taking, blessing and giving that shape this text, amplified by the priestly Melchizedek's use of bread and wine. In truth, there is more going on here than familiar symbolic gestures. When Abram returns from defeating Chedorlaomer, he accomplishes more than just a military victory. This was also a successful rescue operation, and he returns with his nephew – the previously captive Lot. Thus, the blessing that is pronounced is one which calls to mind both the creative and the redemptive power of God.

Breaking bread in the context of the Eucharist (or Holy Communion – please see the introduction, page 11) is always deeply rooted in retelling the story of God's saving relationship with humans. Whether we do it seldom or often, we are always participating in the definitive story of what it means to be freed from captivity. The rescue of Lot, the exodus of the Israelites and the last supper are all events that point towards the God who rescues us from the forces that stand against us. A faithful retelling of that story requires us to honestly name the powers that stand between us and God today. It also requires us to take those powers seriously. The internal powers of addiction, fragile mental or physical health, guilt or resentment all have the ability to keep us in captivity. The external powers of poverty, oppressive or abusive force or social shame all have the ability to make us feel far from God's saving hand. Yet God reconciles Abram and Lot, just as God reconciles heaven and earth through Christ. When we take, bless and give bread and wine, we proclaim with Melchizedek that those forces do not hold final power over us.

> Redeeming God, deliver us from forces malign
> and bring us back into your heart of love. Amen

Rob Glenny

The power of hospitality

Genesis 18:1–6

The Lord appeared to Abraham by the oaks of Mamre, as he sat at the entrance of his tent in the heat of the day. He looked up and saw three men standing near him. When he saw them, he ran from the tent entrance to meet them, and bowed down to the ground. He said, 'My lord, if I find favour with you, do not pass by your servant. Let a little water be brought, and wash your feet, and rest yourselves under the tree. Let me bring a little bread, that you may refresh yourselves, and after that you may pass on – since you have come to your servant.' So they said, 'Do as you have said.' And Abraham hastened into the tent to Sarah, and said, 'Make ready quickly three measures of choice flour, knead it, and make cakes.'

(NRSV)

| Rob Glenny

Reflection

In 2017, as right-wing protesters marched through the city of Birmingham, a mosque in the centre of the city responded by throwing open its doors for the afternoon and hosting a tea party. The place of worship was bedecked in Union flags and bunting, while inside Muslims served their community with tea, coffee and cakes. Everyone was invited to attend and to share conversation with their neighbours, as well as discover a little more about the people who, on the other side of the city, were being demonised.

We may be familiar with Abraham's encounter with these three figures as a picture of hospitality. But what is striking about the detail in this passage is that, like Birmingham Central Mosque, this is a holistic hospitality on offer. Abraham goes the extra mile. Rather than waiting for the three men to find him, instead he runs through the heat of the day away from his tent to meet them. Rather than greeting them as equals, he bows to the ground in humility and service. Rather than simply offering sustenance, Abraham invites the strangers to wash, rest, eat and drink. Rather than giving ordinary food, Abraham gives instruction to provide the best of what he and Sarah have to offer.

The hospitality of a shared meal provides an opportunity to do more than simply eat. A community that breaks bread together, or one which offers radical hospitality to strangers, is providing an opportunity for both holistic refreshment and meaningful encounter.

> Embracing God, meet us in friend and stranger and help our whole being find its rest in you. Amen

| Rob Glenny

Celebrating God's gifts

Exodus 12:17–20

You shall observe the festival of unleavened bread, for on this very day I brought your companies out of the land of Egypt: you shall observe this day throughout your generations as a perpetual ordinance. In the first month, from the evening of the fourteenth day until the evening of the twenty-first day, you shall eat unleavened bread. For seven days no leaven shall be found in your houses; for whoever eats what is leavened shall be cut off from the congregation of Israel, whether an alien or a native of the land. You shall eat nothing leavened; in all your settlements you shall eat unleavened bread. (NRSV)

| Rob Glenny

Reflection

We all observe festivals, both sacred and secular. Traditions are important, such as the carols we sing at Christmas, the flowers we give out on Mothering Sunday or the poppies worn on Armistice Day. So, it turns out, is food. At the heart of most birthday celebrations is cake. When we gather to celebrate Christmas with our family, the question usually is who will cook, and whose version of the meal will it be. We might observe across the Atlantic a similar set of rituals and customs surrounding the celebration of Thanksgiving. In an episode of the US sitcom *Friends*, Monica ends up cooking potatoes four different ways for four different people, just to satisfy a need to replicate their own family traditions.

The Israelites also put food at the heart of their ritual celebration of what it means to be them. The central symbol of unleavened bread calls to mind how Israel was set free from slavery, and the period of seven days in which nothing else should be eaten reminds them that the God who made the heavens and the earth in the same period is the one in whom they live and breathe and have their being.

The two great festivals of Christian life – Easter and Christmas – are also festivals intended to last more than one day. Various traditions celebrate them for different periods, but the point is that celebrating God's gifts to us (including bread that is blessed and broken), shared and expressed in the communities that we are part of, is something that should be both annual and ongoing.

> Giving God, redeem us from forgetting that you are the host of all we celebrate. Amen

Rob Glenny

Ready to respond

Exodus 12:37–39

The Israelites journeyed from Rameses to Succoth, about six hundred thousand men on foot, besides children. A mixed crowd also went up with them, and livestock in great numbers, both flocks and herds. They baked unleavened cakes of the dough that they had brought out of Egypt; it was not leavened, because they were driven out of Egypt and could not wait, nor had they prepared any provisions for themselves.

(NRSV)

| Rob Glenny

Reflection

Immediately after the Israelites share the Passover meal and the tenth plague is sent over Egypt, the people hastily depart from the land of their enslavement. The journey from slavery to freedom is finally beginning. This passage notes two important details as the people set off.

First, the number of Israelites is significant. Joseph arrives in Egypt alone, but now Israel departs with a community of more than 600,000 and great numbers of livestock. Egypt may have been a tough, and sometimes brutal, place to live, but even in a community shaped by forces beyond its control, God is still at work. The exodus is not a sign of God's seemingly random intervention after centuries of hardship, but the culmination of a redeeming work that has been going on for far longer than we realise.

Second, the departure was urgent. The unleavened cake is a symbol of haste and unpreparedness. There was not the time to let it rise. The cake represents Israel – unable to rise to its calling as God's people in Egypt and formed in haste, taking only what it could manage for the journey ahead. Our journey with God is one where we travel light, remembering Jesus' instruction to take only what is necessary and trusting in God's provision. The God who is able to grow a community in hardship and deliver them in trouble is surely also able to provide all that is sufficient for the journey ahead. Here, we see the delightful contrast of a God who has been steadfastly growing and forming a people for hundreds of years, and the immediacy of a God who calls us to follow without delay.

> Eternal God, work through us like yeast through dough, that when you call we may answer without delay. Amen

| Rob Glenny

A hunger for grace

Exodus 16:13–16

> In the evening quails came up and covered the camp; and in the morning there was a layer of dew around the camp. When the layer of dew lifted, there on the surface of the wilderness was a fine flaky substance, as fine as frost on the ground. When the Israelites saw it, they said to one another, 'What is it?' For they did not know what it was. Moses said to them, 'It is the bread that the Lord has given you to eat. This is what the Lord has commanded: "Gather as much of it as each of you needs, an omer to a person according to the number of persons, all providing for those in their own tents."'
>
> (NRSV)

| Rob Glenny

Reflection

I wonder how you give thanks for your food. Do you pray out loud before every meal? Or pause silently before eating in gratitude? Perhaps you hold hands with others, or make the sign of the cross individually. Sitting down to break bread together with others or on your own is an opportunity to cultivate the habit of gratitude. We tend to call that opportunity 'saying grace', which is an odd turn of phrase. But with this passage in Exodus we can see why it is apt. Throughout the Bible, grace is a freely given gift. It is unexpected, uncontrollable and undeserved. Crucially, it is only within God's power to bestow.

For the Israelites in the wilderness, the habit that needed to be learned was reliance on God's provision. The free gift of exactly enough food for the day ahead was a reminder that God provides all that is needed, no more and no less. In unfamiliar terrain and facing an uncertain future, the Israelites were beginning to discover that eating could be an act of worship, both filling them up and deepening their hunger for the God of good gifts.

When the people saw the bread, they asked, 'What is it?', to which we might well respond: it is all that we need; it is the promise that God gives us enough to flourish; it is a reminder of our humility and God's power. We say that is grace.

> Sustaining God, give us hunger for the grace
> that fills us forever. Amen

| Rob Glenny

The splendour of heaven touching earth

Exodus 25:23–30

You shall make a table of acacia wood, two cubits long, one cubit wide, and a cubit and a half high. You shall overlay it with pure gold, and make a moulding of gold round it. You shall make round it a rim a handbreadth wide, and a moulding of gold round the rim. You shall make for it four rings of gold, and fasten the rings to the four corners at its four legs. The rings that hold the poles used for carrying the table shall be close to the rim. You shall make the poles of acacia wood, and overlay them with gold, and the table shall be carried with these. You shall make its plates and dishes for incense, and its flagons and bowls with which to pour drink-offerings; you shall make them of pure gold. And you shall set the bread of the Presence on the table before me always.

(NRSV)

| Rob Glenny

Reflection

The construction of the temple is one of the key events to take place in the second half of Exodus. As is made clear by the sheer volume of gold that is required to construct the table for the bread of the Presence, this is a piece of architecture which has a purpose beyond being simply functional. It was there to convey something that words fall short of describing: the glory of God. The bread itself has a delightful ambiguity in translation, one which can be read in a variety of eucharistic understandings: it means either the bread that *is* the presence of God or the bread that is *in* the presence of God. We don't know for certain.

Both Jews and Christians share a pattern of ritualised breaking of bread, sometimes in surroundings intended to convey God's majestic glory, sometimes in far more humble settings. What matters is not the objects or furnishings in themselves, but what they point us towards. These are moments when we are invited to draw near to the glory of God, to catch a glimpse of the heavenly reality breaking into our own. Like the table in the temple, or the temple itself, this moment of encounter should clothe us as those who are covered and filled with that glory.

God of glory, break through our dull vision and show us the splendour of heaven touching earth. Amen

| Rob Glenny

Discovering the holy in the ordinary

Leviticus 2:1–3

When anyone presents a grain-offering to the Lord, the offering shall be of choice flour; the worshipper shall pour oil on it, and put frankincense on it, and bring it to Aaron's sons the priests. After taking from it a handful of the choice flour and oil, with all its frankincense, the priest shall turn this token portion into smoke on the altar, an offering by fire of pleasing odour to the Lord. And what is left of the grain-offering shall be for Aaron and his sons, a most holy part of the offerings by fire to the Lord.

(NRSV)

| Rob Glenny

Reflection

The book of Leviticus begins with a series of instructions on how to make appropriate offerings to the Lord. It can sometimes be difficult to find in these passages immediate relevance to our living, but perhaps there is more here than we realise.

Christina Rossetti's memorable poem 'In the bleak midwinter' ends by pondering what might be an adequate gift for the almighty God who takes human form. The words are probably familiar from the hymn:

> *What can I give Him, poor as I am?*
> *If I were a shepherd, I would bring a lamb;*
> *If I were a Wise Man, I would do my part;*
> *Yet what I can I give Him: give my heart.*

We call those words to mind at Christmas, but perhaps we should ponder them at other times of the year. In this offering, the people are not expected to offer what they do not possess, but instead *anyone* can bring a grain-offering of choice flour. This is what sanctification looks like – offering to God the best that we have of the most ordinary of things and discovering the ways in which God can make it holy.

If we are serious about God transforming the gifts that we have to offer, then we need both the humility to recognise that they are profoundly ordinary parts of our being and the courage to offer the very best of those parts. Breaking bread in God's presence reminds us of both of those realities and of the God whose incarnation is the very act of sanctifying our ordinary being.

> Sanctifying God, teach us to value the ways we are ordinary, and through them transform us into holy people. Amen

| Rob Glenny

The fellowship of brokenness and weakness

Joshua 9:8–9, 11–14

They said to Joshua, 'We are your servants.' And Joshua said to them, 'Who are you? And where do you come from?' They said to him, 'Your servants have come from a very far country, because of the name of the Lord your God; for we have heard a report of him, of all that he did in Egypt... So our elders and all the inhabitants of our country said to us, "Take provisions in your hand for the journey; go to meet them, and say to them, 'We are your servants; come now, make a treaty with us.'" Here is our bread; it was still warm when we took it from our houses as our food for the journey, on the day we set out to come to you, but now, see, it is dry and mouldy; these wineskins were new when we filled them, and see, they are burst; and these garments and sandals of ours are worn out from the very long journey.' So the leaders partook of their provisions, and did not ask direction from the Lord.

(NRSV)

| Rob Glenny

Reflection

Concerned for their safety, the Gibeonites come to meet Joshua with an act of deception. The mouldy bread and the burst wineskins are intended to convey that they had travelled from a far-off land, when in fact they were living nearby the Israelites. Conned, Joshua and the leaders do not consult the Lord, but instead share their provisions and make a peace treaty with the Gibeonites.

What we see in this passage depends which side we read it from. From the point of view of Joshua and the Israelites, this could be taken as a straightforward condemnation for not involving God in important decisions. But read it again through the eyes of the Gibeonites and an alternative perspective can be seen. The Gibeonites recognise their own weakness and vulnerability compared to the might of the Israelites. They may be overstating their weakness in how they present themselves, but we can treat their greeting (that they come as servants because they have heard reports of the power of the Lord) with sincerity. A posture of humility is rewarded not just with immediate safety, but with peace and fellowship and food, as the Israelites share what they have.

Remember your weakness in the presence of God and God's people as you seek their fellowship and break bread with them.

Gracious God, give us courage to confess our weakness and arms to embrace the weakness of others. Amen

Rob Glenny

The abundance of God

Ruth 2:14–17

At mealtime Boaz said to her, 'Come here, and eat some of this bread, and dip your morsel in the sour wine.' So she sat beside the reapers, and he heaped up for her some parched grain. She ate until she was satisfied, and she had some left over. When she got up to glean, Boaz instructed his young men, 'Let her glean even among the standing sheaves, and do not reproach her. You must also pull out some handfuls for her from the bundles, and leave them for her to glean, and do not rebuke her.' So she gleaned in the field until evening. Then she beat out what she had gleaned, and it was about an ephah of barley.

(NRSV)

| Rob Glenny

Reflection

Naomi and Ruth's situation is pretty hopeless as they travel to a foreign country, bereaved and alone. In a deeply patriarchal culture, the protection and provision of their family was the key to survival, but theirs is lost. So, at the mercy of others, Ruth goes to the fields, hoping to gather a little of what is left behind by Boaz and his reapers.

What follows is an extraordinary act of generosity between Jew and Gentile. Boaz allows Ruth not only to glean the little of what is left behind, but also to share in the food and wine that the workers consume, and then to take all that she requires from the field without reproach. As ever, the little details illuminate the story. Ruth eats until she is satisfied, but there is still food left over. Just as with the miracle of water and wine, the feeding of the thousands or the miraculous catch of fish, the end result is that there is enough to satisfy but far more left over. God's modus operandi is not to satisfy but to overflow with abundance.

Another salient detail is given at the end of the previous chapter – all this takes place in Bethlehem (which in Hebrew means House of Bread). We are reminded that this will be the place where God will make the definitive act of generous love. Through Jesus, God becomes as vulnerable as Ruth in the Bethlehem fields and goes on to be known in the breaking of bread. We remember as we eat that physical bread will satisfy us for a short time, but the overflowing, abundant generosity of God will fill us forever, and there will always be more left over.

God of abundant love, nourish us with the faith that deepens our hunger for you. Amen

| Rob Glenny

Responding to God's call

1 Samuel 10:3–7

'Then you shall go on from there further and come to the oak of Tabor; three men going up to God at Bethel will meet you there, one carrying three kids, another carrying three loaves of bread, and another carrying a skin of wine. They will greet you and give you two loaves of bread, which you shall accept from them. After that you shall come to Gibeath-elohim, at the place where the Philistine garrison is; there, as you come to the town, you will meet a band of prophets coming down from the shrine with harp, tambourine, flute, and lyre playing in front of them; they will be in a prophetic frenzy. Then the spirit of the Lord will possess you, and you will be in a prophetic frenzy along with them and be turned into a different person. Now when these signs meet you, do whatever you see fit to do, for God is with you.'

(NRSV)

Reflection

This set of instructions comes immediately as Samuel anoints Saul, Israel's first king. With a new vocation to fulfil, Saul sets off towards Gilgal. It's an interesting location, which recalls the end of the Israelites' wilderness wandering and will also be the place that marks Saul's rebellion against God and the beginning of the end of his reign. When the Israelites end their journey through the desert, this is also the moment at which the manna from heaven ceases to appear for them. The symbolic action of the two loaves of bread being handed over shows Saul being given all that he requires as he begins this new phase of Israel's history.

Saul is changing vocation or, if you prefer, responding in the moment to God's call upon his life. This passage gives us an early indication of a couple of the things we might reflect upon when we are at a crossroads in life and have important decisions to make. First, as Saul does alongside Samuel, have you tested your decision in the community of the faithful? Second, as the spirit of the Lord descends upon Saul and he is changed, are you open to the prompting of the Holy Spirit and ready to allow God to be at work in every part of your decision? How might an act of breaking bread – on your own or as part of a service at church – help with this?

Steadfast God, send your Spirit upon us, that all of who we are may be in companionship with you. Amen

| Derek Tidball

No ordinary bread

1 Samuel 21:3–6a

'Now then, what do you have on hand? Give me five loaves of bread, or whatever you can find.' But the priest answered David, 'I don't have any ordinary bread to hand; however, there is some consecrated bread here – provided the men have kept themselves from women.' David replied, 'Indeed women have been kept from us, as usual whenever I set out. The men's bodies are holy even on missions that are not holy. How much more so today!' So the priest gave him the consecrated bread...

(NIV)

| Derek Tidball

Reflection

David is on the run from Saul and in desperate need of food for himself and his unseen army. He knows there will be bread in the shrine at Nob, but when he asks for supplies, Abimelek, the priest, is suspicious. The only bread available is special, consecrated bread, usually reserved for priests alone. But David, not knowing where Abimelek's loyalties lie, spins a yarn about being on a secret mission for Saul. Moreover, he claims his men are worthy of the consecrated bread because, even though they are on a dirty mission, they have led consecrated lives while on the mission and have abstained from sex. Abimelek gives him the loaves and immediately replaces them with bread fresh from the oven.

We might be puzzled by this story except that Jesus retells it in Matthew 12:3–4, in an argument about sabbath regulations. Jesus does not criticise David's behaviour, but uses the incident to teach his disciples that compassionate action is more important in God's eyes than sticking to religious rules. Feeding the hungry far outweighs law-bound religious practices. In a world of immense hunger, we have no excuse for missing the point. Thank God for those who have understood that and feed the hungry in Christ's name.

It may have happened in a somewhat unorthodox way, but at Nob God provided for David's need and gave him his 'daily bread'. The same God, the source of all good things, can sustain us in our need, too, and not just in terms of physical hunger.

> Reflect on God's generous provision in your life and in particular for the provision of daily bread.

Derek Tidball

Thinking about who you break bread with

1 Kings 13:7–10

The king said to the man of God, 'Come home with me for a meal, and I will give you a gift.' But the man of God answered the king, 'Even if you were to give me half your possessions, I would not go with you, nor would I eat bread or drink water here. For I was commanded by the word of the Lord: "You must not eat bread or drink water or return by the way you came."' So he took another road and did not return by the way he had come to Bethel.

(NIV)

| Derek Tidball

Reflection

King Jeroboam led God's people astray. When Jeroboam seeks to silence the prophet God sent to rebuke him, his arm shrivels. Like others when desperate, he asks God for a favour. When the prophet prays for him, he is healed. The king then invites the prophet home for supper and offers him a reward. It's a natural way to say thank you, but the king is also seeking to co-opt the prophet to serve his corrupt religious cause. The prophet wisely refuses, because God had commanded him to return home without accepting any hospitality, which he does. Sadly, the prophet doesn't maintain his obedience to God, as 1 Kings 13 later reveals. He is eventually compromised by an old prophet, with disastrous consequences.

From the Psalms to Paul's letters, we're often warned to be careful about who we associate with closely. Alongside this, we have the example of Jesus, who ate with the ostracised (see, for example, Matthew 9:11) and broke bread with one who would deny him and another who would betray him.

Breaking bread and eating together are signs of friendship in both Jewish and Christian cultures. The contrasting examples of association above and the text from 1 Kings challenge us to think how we can offer friendship through eating together and breaking bread, while maintaining fidelity to the Lord.

> Lord, grant me wisdom in my friendships and keep me faithful in my following of Jesus. Amen

| Derek Tidball

Extraordinary grace

1 Kings 17:8–12

Then the word of the Lord came to [Elijah]:
'Go at once to Zarephath in the region
of Sidon and stay there. I have instructed a
widow there to supply you with food.' So he went
to Zarephath. When he came to the town gate,
a widow was there gathering sticks. He called
to her and asked, 'Would you bring me a little
water in a jar so I may have a drink?' As she was
going to get it, he called, 'And bring me, please,
a piece of bread.' 'As surely as the Lord your God
lives,' she replied, 'I don't have any bread – only
a handful of flour in a jar and a little olive oil in a
jug. I am gathering a few sticks to take home and
make a meal for myself and my son, that we may
eat it – and die.'

(NIV)

| Derek Tidball

Reflection

Having prophesied a drought, Elijah falls victims to it himself. So God commands him to travel outside Israel, to meet with a widow who will care for him.

The incident demonstrates God's providential care. The God of the universe takes care to provide for his prophet and does so by arranging a meeting with a widow far from home. Apparently chance meetings sometimes turn out to be divine appointments. It also highlights God's inclusive love. The widow isn't an Israelite worshipper and Zarephath is a Phoenician city. When Jesus refers to this story (Luke 4:25–26), it is to point out that God's grace is not exclusive to the Jews. Furthermore, while she turns out to be desperate because her larder is empty, God turns out to be faithful. He works a miracle, taking her little and turning it into much.

George Muller, who established orphanages in Bristol in the 1830s, had no reliable source of income. They often wouldn't know how God was going to feed them. But he did, often miraculously. In one crisis, Muller commented, 'I was not looking at *the little in hand, but at the fullness of God.*' That's what Elijah did, and the widow – and God provided. Perhaps we're sometimes too self-sufficient to see God at work.

> Thank you, Lord, that your grace makes room even for me. Forgive my self-sufficiency, and teach me to depend more on you for my daily bread. Amen

When will we ever learn?

Psalm 78:22–25

For they did not believe in God or trust in his deliverance. Yet he gave a command to the skies above and opened the doors of the heavens; he rained down manna for the people to eat, he gave them the grain of heaven. Human beings ate the bread of angels; he sent them all the food they could eat.

(NIV)

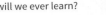

Reflection

Since God performed many miracles in releasing Israel from oppression in Egypt and provided for them in the initial stages of their wilderness journey, you would think it would be easy for them to trust God. Yet instead of expressing gratitude, they grumble. Instead of belief, they opt for doubt. In spite of his anger at this, God again works a miracle and provides them with manna and quails to eat daily. It is 'the bread of angels'. True to his character, he 'rains' the food down on them, not giving grudgingly but generously. Such is God's mercy, patience and grace.

It's easy to criticise the Israelites. When would they ever learn? How many signs did they need before they started trusting God? Yet the moment we voice such criticism, an inner voice reminds us how readily we default to questioning and grumbling rather than trusting and thanking. Has not God proved himself to us over and over again? And yet, perhaps, even today, we find it hard to trust him and somehow think we are better than he is at managing our lives.

Practise thankfulness. Doing so regularly will make it a healthy, holy habit. You could simply break and eat a piece of bread as you do this. Thankfulness benefits us and saves us from negative living. It furnishes a true perspective and balance in life, even as we face its challenges. It benefits others who may be weary of our complaining and makes us easier companions. Supremely, it honours God and gives him no more than he deserves as a generous, loving provider of all we need. As the old hymn advised: 'Count your blessings, name them one by one, and it will surprise you what the Lord has done' (Johnson Oatman, 1856–1922).

Spend time today listing some of the causes of gratitude you have for God's provision in your life, including the bread you break.

| Derek Tidball

God's environmental policy

Psalm 104:10–14

> He makes springs pour water into the ravines; it flows between the mountains. They give water to all the beasts of the field; the wild donkeys quench their thirst. The birds of the sky nest by the waters; they sing among the branches. He waters the mountains from his upper chambers; the land is satisfied by the fruit of his work. He makes grass grow for the cattle, and plants for people to cultivate – bringing forth food from the earth.
>
> (NIV)

| Derek Tidball

Reflection

We are increasingly concerned about global warming and what we are doing to the environment, and rightly so. Yet there is a more fundamental truth about the environment which saves us from fear while encouraging us to act responsibly. It's not our environmental policy – it's God's.

When God created the earth, he made it to function in a certain sustainable way. Springs deep in the earth and rain from high in the sky provide the necessary water to irrigate crops and plants. Provision is made for all living creatures. The psalmist also rejoices that creation is more than merely functional – it is also bountiful. Birds sing songs of praise and, in the verse that follows our reading, it is said that wine 'gladdens human hearts'.

Planet earth is richly resourced. Our responsibility is to manage it properly and to share its produce with those in need. God has ensured that we have enough for all our needs, if not for our greed. How absurd that one-third of the world goes hungry daily, while another third suffer from over-eating. Far from encouraging self-satisfied enjoyment and over-indulgence, the words of this psalm encourage us to fall in line with God's design and intention for all of his creation and his creatures.

Generous God, whenever I break bread, may I rejoice in your generous provision for my needs and learn from you how to share with those who are hungry. Help us to manage your creation with care. Amen

| Derek Tidball

A different kind of diet

Proverbs 4:14–17

Do not set foot on the path of the wicked or walk in the way of evildoers. Avoid it, do not travel on it; turn from it and go on your way. For they cannot rest until they do evil; they are robbed of sleep till they make someone stumble. They eat the bread of wickedness and drink the wine of violence.

(NIV)

| Derek Tidball

Reflection

The philosopher Ludwig Feuerbach said, 'A man is what he eats.' While it is not the whole truth, there is truth in the maxim. Living on fast food may give immediate pleasure but is no basis for healthy, long-term living. Eat fatty, sugar-laden food and we become sluggish and overweight. Eat healthily, without over-indulging, and we become energetic. Moreover, we develop an appetite for certain kinds and quantities of food. What we crave is usually shaped by the food habits we have cultivated.

Proverbs picks up both those issues when it uses food as a metaphor for what nourishes our wider life. Today's reading warns us against a regular diet consisting of ignoring God's pattern for living and behaving badly towards others. If that's our diet, we not only live foolishly, causing ourselves all sorts of unnecessary grief in life, but we distance ourselves from God and end up facing ultimate judgement and destruction. In addition, the more we eat this unhealthy diet, the more we crave evil, so that we 'cannot rest' until we have it. Wrongdoing becomes addictive and eventually fatal, unless we change our diets.

Half of my friends seem to be on perpetual diets. They watch what they eat carefully, counting their calorie intake, resisting carbohydrates, measuring portion quantities or ensuring plenty of fruit and veg, depending on which diet they're on. Are we as careful to ensure our spiritual and moral diets are as healthy? Regularly digesting the words of the Bible leads to true spiritual health and helps us avoid the 'bread of wickedness'.

Review your way of life and see whether it is time to change your spiritual diet in order to healthily enjoy God and his design for life. What part might the regular breaking of bread play in this?

| Derek Tidball

The blessing of moderation

Proverbs 30:7–9

'Two things I ask of you, Lord; do not refuse me before I die: keep falsehood and lies far from me; give me neither poverty nor riches, but give me only my daily bread. Otherwise, I may have too much and disown you and say, "Who is the Lord?" Or I may become poor and steal, and so dishonour the name of my God.' (NIV)

Reflection

It's easy to recognise the evil of extreme hunger, even if it is far from our experience. Tales from the past often concern those whose poverty drove them to steal in order to survive, only to incur severe penalties imposed by those who had plenty. We all admire Oliver Twist asking for more to stave off his hunger. Sadly, this isn't only in the past, is it? Many homeless people are condemned to searching through litter bins and supermarket skips to find scraps on which to live, even in prosperous countries. Globally, the picture is even worse. The wise man prays here that he won't be put in that position but will have enough food to stop him having to break the law.

But do we recognise the opposite problem: that of having too much, which can lead us to arrogant self-sufficiency and dispensing with the need for God? We get used to buying whatever we want, sometimes resulting in buying too much and becoming wasteful. We assume we've earned the right to such plenty and so completely ignore the God who has provided for us. When Jesus taught us to pray for our daily bread (Matthew 6:11), he was teaching us how utterly dependent on God we still are.

So many thoughts arise from today's reading. It points to the need for compassion towards those who do not have much and thankfulness for what we do have. Do we still say grace at meals? It encourages us to be honest and God-centred, whatever our circumstances in life. It implies that we shouldn't be wasteful when we have plenty. And, above all, it encourages us to acknowledge the blessing of moderation in all things.

Are there ways you can adjust your lifestyle to avoid falling into the temptations of having too little or too much? How might the holy habit of breaking bread, practised regularly, help achieve this balance?

| Derek Tidball

Tempting, threatening, treacherous words

Isaiah 36:16b–18

'This is what the king of Assyria says: make peace with me and come out to me. Then each of you will eat fruit from your own vine and fig-tree and drink water from your own cistern, until I come and take you to a land like your own – a land of corn and new wine, a land of bread and vineyards. Do not let Hezekiah mislead you when he says, "The Lord will deliver us." Have the gods of any nations ever delivered their lands from the hand of the king of Assyria?'

(NIV)

| Derek Tidball

Reflection

When, in 703BC, King Hezekiah asserted independence against the superpower of Assyria, Sennacherib inevitably moved against him. One tactic he adopted was to cause disaffection between the citizens of Jerusalem and their king. Sennacherib's commander offered them a better deal than they were going to get if they remained stubborn in their rebellion. His offer, broadcast to the city in their own language, was tempting – note the inclusion of bread and wine in what is offered. In the short term, they'd enjoy the comfort of their own homes and produce. But that velvet glove hid an iron fist. After that, they would, like everyone else Assyria conquered, be deported. Try as he might to say they'd go to a land like their own, they would still be in exile. The words were threatening.

But worse was to come. In a direct assault on their faith in the power of their God, the Assyrian told them that resistance was useless because their God was incapable of delivering them. He was inviting them to act treacherously towards Yahweh.

Little did Sennacherib know Israel's God! Eventually his army was destroyed, its remnant retreated and Sennacherib was assassinated by his sons.

Sennacherib's voice was essentially the same as Satan's in Eden. Eve listened to it and went for the attractive but forbidden fruit. It's often tempting to go for the easy, short-term option in our moral and spiritual lives. It often seems the only realistic path. In reality, it is spiritual treachery. It is rebelling against the God who has poured grace into our lives. Rather, whatever the problem, persevering trust in God, who can *and does* deliver, yields unimagined miracles.

> 'Lead us not into temptation, but deliver
> us from the evil one' (Matthew 6:13).
> May your true bread nurture and sustain us.

Life-giving bread

Isaiah 55:1–2

| Derek Tidball

'Come, all you who are thirsty, come to the waters; and you who have no money, come, buy and eat! Come, buy wine and milk without money and without cost. Why spend money on what is not bread, and your labour on what does not satisfy? Listen, listen to me, and eat what is good, and you will delight in the richest of fare.'

(NIV)

| Derek Tidball

Reflection

Within a mile of my home there are five major supermarkets. Their shelves groan and their offers all cry out, 'Buy me, buy me!' Consequently, it's hard to identify with the pictures of hardship we sometimes see on the news when people in famine-stricken areas scramble over each other to get a bowl of rice or some bottles of water from a relief agency. Yet, that's more like the situation Isaiah addresses. Middle Eastern lands were often parched and struggled with very poor harvests. There was a desperate need to quench people's thirst and fill their empty stomachs with life-giving bread. But how?

Through Isaiah, God paints a picture of the spiritual desolation Israel has suffered in the exile, but he promises them that a new day of grace is dawning, when he will freely remedy their ills and rebuild their nation. The remedy is not without cost, but he will foot the bill himself, rather than charge it to them.

Three things are necessary for it to happen. One: as with any invitation, they need to accept it. Two: they need to put all their store on this invitation and not look to other solutions, whether political or religious. These may look attractive but will prove a false economy, wasting their merger resources. Three: responding involves listening, not only to God's invitation but also to all his other wisdom and instructions, so that they might begin to live again.

Jesus updated the invitation: 'I am the bread of life. Whoever comes to me will never go hungry, and whoever believes in me will never be thirsty' (John 6:35). He awaits our RSVP.

> Lord, teach me to listen to you and feed on you,
> the bread of life. Amen

| Derek Tidball

The bread of sorrow

Jeremiah 16:5–7 (abridged)

For this is what the Lord says: 'Do not enter a house where there is a funeral meal; do not go to mourn or show sympathy, because I have withdrawn my blessing, my love and my pity from this people,' declares the Lord. 'Both high and low will die in this land... No one will offer food to comfort those who mourn for the dead – not even for a father or a mother – nor will anyone give them a drink to console them.' (NIV)

| Derek Tidball

Reflection

We speak about – and, let's be honest, often indulge in – comfort eating. When we're weary or feeling low, we have a quick fix to lift us up. But in these harsh words, God bans the prophet Jeremiah from any comfort eating. He is forbidden from even taking part in the usual customs of mourning and is instructed to absent himself from the normal courtesies associated with grief. Why?

It is God's way of driving home the seriousness of the plight Judah is facing. Having ignored God for so long, lived lives that rode roughshod over their covenant with him and stubbornly refused to change their ways, Judah has exhausted God's patience. Judah will shortly experience his anger, as the nation is destroyed and its people taken into exile for 70 years. Jeremiah will join them there. To feast at such a time would be like the orchestra playing on while the Titanic was sinking. It would be nothing more than a foolish distraction and denial of reality. It would be applying a sticking plaster when drastic surgery was needed.

Most of our readings have celebrated God's abundant provision and encouraged us to share with those who have little. This passage is altogether different, like the reverse thrust of an aircraft about to land. Neither Judah nor we can glibly presume on God's goodness, on business as usual. His grace is not 'cheap grace', to use Dietrich Bonhoeffer's phrase. There is a time when we have to face up to our failures and sin and express our repentance in tangible form. The bread we break as followers of Jesus reminds us of both our sinfulness and God's grace. Both realities are present – and thankfully grace prevails.

> When you break bread, what does the sacramental act say to you about sinfulness and grace, about sorrow and joy?

| Naomi Starkey

Making space for grace

Matthew 4:1–4

> Then Jesus was led by the Spirit into the wilderness to be tempted by the devil. After fasting for forty days and forty nights, he was hungry. The tempter came to him and said, 'If you are the Son of God, tell these stones to become bread.' Jesus answered, 'It is written: "Man shall not live on bread alone, but on every word that comes from the mouth of God."' (NIV)

Naomi Starkey

Reflection

The story of Jesus' temptation in the wilderness comes straight after his baptism, when he was filled with the Holy Spirit and heard from God himself that he was indeed the 'beloved Son'. This dramatic affirmation is then subjected to rigorous testing: 'Are you really the Son of God? Go ahead and prove it!'

We might find it strange that it's the Holy Spirit who leads Jesus into the wilderness, which turns out to be a place of such arduous challenge. 'Going on retreat' can sound like a bit of 'chill time', but Jesus' wilderness weeks have more of a battleground feel. He has yet to start his public ministry; it's crucial that he has tested his calling as rigorously as possible. Through his temptations, he proves that using his God-given power must only be for kingdom purposes, not for personal gratification.

Fasting as a Christian spiritual discipline has had a resurgence in recent years, particularly during Lent. It can be stereotyped as 'bodily mortification', but the focus is really on laying aside our usual routines to make space for encounter with God. Traditionally, people have sometimes fasted before attending a Eucharist (or service of Holy Communion) and, as with fasting during Lent, this is about abstinence rather than self-starvation, placing spiritual nourishment above physical appetite.

In the developed world, most people suffer from too much, rather than too little, food; we speak of 'living in a consumer culture'. 'Feeding the soul' can easily fall towards the bottom of our priorities. The Eucharist shows us that 'food' means so much more than how we fill our stomachs and what delights our taste buds. We're invited to God's table and fed with the bread of heaven – and then we're sent out to invite others.

> If you decided to commit to a time of fasting, what would you find hardest to give up and why? If you have any doubts about fasting, do discuss this with your doctor.

| Naomi Starkey

Thanks for gifts received

Matthew 7:7–9, 11

'Ask and it will be given to you; seek and you will find; knock and the door will be opened to you. For everyone who asks receives; the one who seeks finds; and to the one who knocks, the door will be opened. Which of you, if your son asks for bread, will give him a stone?... If you, then, though you are evil, know how to give good gifts to your children, how much more will your Father in heaven give good gifts to those who ask him!'

(NIV)

| Naomi Starkey

Reflection

In this passage from his sermon on the mount, Jesus draws on the expectations of happy family relationships to explain how our 'Father in heaven' relates to his earthly children. Reassuringly, he points out that what would seem preposterous to any loving (yet inevitably flawed and faulty) parent is even more preposterous from Father God's perspective. 'Ask, seek, knock,' he tells his listeners, 'and of course he will hear you. Of course he will provide what you need.'

Some Christians are uncomfortable with the word 'Eucharist,' yet it simply comes from the Greek for 'thanksgiving'. In the many different versions of the prayer used to consecrate the bread and wine, the recurring theme is praise and thanksgiving to God for his gifts to his people. Chief of these gifts is, of course, salvation through his Son, in remembrance of whose death we take, eat and drink.

Occasionally, I hear complaints about 'excessive liturgy' – that the Anglican Church (which I serve as a priest) uses too many words around what is essentially a simple act. Of course, it's important to take note of the age and attention span of congregations, but we also need regular reminding of the significance of what we share in the Eucharist. Well-crafted liturgy draws us together to share the story of Jesus' sacrifice and opens us, together, to the extraordinary generosity of our heavenly Father.

If, for whatever reason, we doubt our own ability to 'give good gifts to our children', how might that limit our understanding of God's longing to give to us?

Naomi Starkey

Getting it wrong

Mark 8:14–17, 19–21 (abridged)

The disciples had forgotten to bring bread, except for one loaf they had with them in the boat. 'Be careful,' Jesus warned them. 'Watch out for the yeast of the Pharisees and that of Herod.' They discussed this with one another and said, 'It is because we have no bread'... Jesus asked them: 'Why are you talking about having no bread?... When I broke the five loaves for the five thousand, how many basketfuls of pieces did you pick up?' 'Twelve,' they replied. 'And when I broke the seven loaves for the four thousand, how many basketfuls of pieces did you pick up?' They answered, 'Seven.' He said to them, 'Do you still not understand?'

(NIV)

| Naomi Starkey

Reflection

This rather cryptic little episode is characteristic of Mark's gospel in its emphasis on the disciples' lack of understanding. Together with Jesus, they're leaving Galilee after two crowd-feeding miracles, en route for Judea and eventually Jerusalem.

Whereas bread in scripture usually symbolises the basics or what is necessary for life, yeast (an essential ingredient for most bread) is a more ambiguous symbol, an unseen influence that works sometimes for good but usually not so. Jesus is warning his friends about the influence of the religious (Pharisees) and political (Herod) elites against God's kingdom, but they assume he's telling them off for lack of foresight on the catering front.

As elsewhere in Mark, we hear Jesus' frustration at the disciples' inability to see God's power at work through his words and deeds. They have to be alert to the human agendas that could make it even harder for them to grasp the spiritual truths he is trying to teach them.

Sadly, the Eucharist has often been a focus for inter-church disagreement: what we call it (see the introduction, page 11), how exactly and how often we celebrate it, who is and isn't allowed to receive it, what precisely happens during the prayer of consecration, and so on. We think we understand (and that we're right), but we don't really (and we may be wrong). We must work hard to stay aware of assumptions and prejudices that might cloud our thinking and prevent us from seeing God at work.

> Pray that what binds us together as God's children remains stronger than all that would drive us apart.

| Naomi Starkey

Jesus' last Passover

Mark 14:12b–16

Jesus' disciples asked him, 'Where do you want us to go and make preparations for you to eat the Passover?' So he sent two of his disciples, telling them, 'Go into the city, and a man carrying a jar of water will meet you. Follow him. Say to the owner of the house he enters, "The Teacher asks: where is my guest room, where I may eat the Passover with my disciples?" He will show you a large room upstairs, furnished and ready. Make preparations for us there.' The disciples left, went into the city and found things just as Jesus had told them. So they prepared the Passover.

(NIV)

| Naomi Starkey

Reflection

Here, Mark reminds us of the setting for the last supper: the annual Passover meal commemorating the escape of God's people from Egypt. Jesus will take this tradition and remake it to commemorate his own death, which will bring people to freedom just as Moses led the Israelites to freedom centuries before. Jesus' death will also create a new community under a new covenant, saved by the shed blood of God himself, instead of the lambs slain to take the place of the firstborn (see Exodus 12).

Jesus is no helpless victim, however. He chooses to be 'led like a lamb to the slaughter' (Isaiah 53:7), so that no more helpless lambs need die, futilely, to atone for sins that will be committed again and again. All human violence will be absorbed into and paid for by the violent death to which Jesus will submit himself.

There is an air of intrigue about this passage, with the disciples told to follow the mysterious water-carrier (a man doing what was traditionally women's work) and receiving what amounts to a password guaranteeing access to the pre-prepared 'upper room'. Jesus is making ready for the most important night of his life so far, against a backdrop of escalating hostility from the religious authorities.

This central act of our faith has been and continues to be celebrated in all manner of places, from the grandest of cathedrals to the improvised altars of the battlefield, from packed sports stadia to hidden gatherings of secret believers. Whatever the liturgical style and public prominence, it retains at its heart the intimacy of a meal shared with friends.

> When you next receive the Eucharist, do so holding before God a situation of ongoing hostility somewhere in the world – and pray that Jesus' saving death may bring freedom from violence even there.

Naomi Starkey

Bread and betrayal

Mark 14:17–21

When evening came, Jesus arrived with the Twelve. While they were reclining at the table eating, he said, 'Truly I tell you, one of you will betray me – one who is eating with me.' They were saddened, and one by one they said to him, 'Surely you don't mean me?' 'It is one of the Twelve,' he replied, 'one who dips bread into the bowl with me. The Son of Man will go just as it is written about him. But woe to that man who betrays the Son of Man! It would be better for him if he had not been born.' (NIV)

| Naomi Starkey

Reflection

Jesus has gathered with his closest friends for their meal of remembrance and celebration – and then comes his shocking warning of betrayal. The disciples would have known about the growing tension between Jesus and the authorities, but could one of their inner circle actually betray their beloved teacher? Poignantly, we know the answer to their appalled questioning: 'Surely you don't mean me?' There's the shock, too, of realising that Judas was present at the table; we're not told that he left before the bread is broken and the wine poured.

In many churches, receiving the Eucharist is restricted to members (however membership is judged); the idea of an 'open table' – access to the bread and wine for everyone who wishes to receive – is a matter of debate. While any institution needs some rules and boundaries in order to flourish, the question of who should and should not receive the Eucharist is not necessarily straightforward in practice.

What about the unbaptised seeker who turns up at a service, wants to join in and feels deeply moved by taking Communion? What about the church member who is known to some as a malicious gossip and troublemaker, yet comes forward week after week? According to the rules of many churches, the former should not have received, while the latter is free to do so.

However our church life is arranged, we do well to remember that (like baptism) the Eucharist is a gift of God and not something we can ever deserve. Our rules and liturgies should reflect this truth.

How can our churches best express the hospitality of the Eucharist, the family meal to which all are invited?

Naomi Starkey

This is for you

Mark 14:22–26

While they were eating, Jesus took bread, and when he had given thanks, he broke it and gave it to his disciples, saying, 'Take it; this is my body.' Then he took a cup, and when he had given thanks, he gave it to them, and they all drank from it. 'This is my blood of the covenant, which is poured out for many,' he said to them. 'Truly I tell you, I will not drink again from the fruit of the vine until that day when I drink it new in the kingdom of God.' When they had sung a hymn, they went out to the Mount of Olives.

(NIV)

Reflection

The Passover involved four cups of wine between the different courses of the meal, with corresponding words of blessing and explanation, so Jesus gives new meaning to a familiar format. The covenant between God and Israel was sealed in blood, and now Jesus identifies the Passover wine with his blood, which would be shed just hours thence, sealing the new covenant between God and all people.

By taking, eating and drinking, the disciples (and we) are not 'eating up Jesus' but taking his atoning death into our bodies, making it (literally as well as spiritually) a means of life. We eat and drink to stay alive physically; we eat and drink the consecrated bread and wine to connect ourselves afresh with Jesus' saving act on the cross.

Jesus' friends probably did not understand his words about 'not drinking again from the fruit of the vine'. We hear them as a reference to his resurrection, and they remind us, too, that the Eucharist is not only a memorial of Jesus' death but also a celebration of that resurrection – and an anticipation of the heavenly banquet to which God invites every one of his children.

After that profound moment in the upper room, Mark returns to the real-life drama of that night. The gathering finishes with a suitable hymn and the group leaves for the Mount of Olives, making their way to an olive orchard by name of Gethsemane – but Judas knows where they are headed.

How often do you reflect on the Eucharist as a foretaste of God's kingdom feast?

| Naomi Starkey

Praying like Jesus

Luke 11:1–4

One day Jesus was praying in a certain place. When he finished, one of his disciples said to him, 'Lord, teach us to pray, just as John taught his disciples.' He said to them, 'When you pray, say: "Father, hallowed be your name, your kingdom come. Give us each day our daily bread. Forgive us our sins, for we also forgive everyone who sins against us. And lead us not into temptation."'

(NIV)

Reflection

The words of this prayer are so familiar – and so often introduced with words to the effect of 'Let us pray as Jesus himself taught us' – that we can overlook the wonder of it. This is the Son of God teaching his followers how to pray to his Father. These are the kind of things we should say to God himself, and, as we do so, we are following the example of Jesus.

Praise comes before petition, reminding us whom we are addressing: not a generalised higher power or anonymous god, but the one we know as Father. And it is Father whom we ask for daily bread, echoing Jesus' teaching in Matthew 7 and Luke 11, where he tells his listeners how the Father delights to supply their needs, more so than any earthly father.

Apparently the phrase about daily bread should be translated as, 'Carry on giving us our bread each day', and the bread here is usually understood as daily needs and what we need to keep us going, rather than a specific loaf of bread. Jewish thought didn't divide the world into physical and spiritual in the way we tend to, however, and we do well to remember that we can ask God to supply whatever we need to keep us going each day, whether a loaf of bread or a dose of courage.

Having the Eucharist at the heart of our regular worship is an essential reminder that ours is an embodied faith. We don't just think about the sacrifice of Christ's body; we eat and drink it. Doing so, we ask the Father, though his Spirit, to feed us so that we are strong enough to resist temptation, to forgive others and to bear daily witness to his grace.

Lord, teach me to pray.

| Naomi Starkey

At table together

Luke 24:28–32

As they approached the village to which they were going, Jesus continued on as if he were going further. But they urged him strongly, 'Stay with us, for it is nearly evening; the day is almost over.' So he went in to stay with them. When he was at the table with them, he took bread, gave thanks, broke it and began to give it to them. Then their eyes were opened and they recognised him, and he disappeared from their sight. They asked each other, 'Were not our hearts burning within us while he talked with us on the road and opened the Scriptures to us?'   (NIV)

Reflection

This is the final scene of another beautifully told episode from Luke, gospel-writer and master storyteller. As Easter Day draws to a close, two disconsolate disciples are homeward-bound, disbelieving of the morning's momentous events. Jesus himself comes up (unrecognised by them) and explains 'what was said in all the Scriptures concerning himself' (v. 27). The disciples urge him to stay with them overnight (the origin of the hymn 'Abide with me'), and they start sharing food together.

As they suddenly realise who it is that is breaking bread for them, Jesus disappears. The two he leaves behind, though, are no longer disconsolate but so radiant with excitement and joy that they rush back to Jerusalem, find the rest of Jesus' followers and pour out the story of what has happened (vv. 33–35). Thus the community of disciples is further strengthened, another step in readying them for the transforming power of the day of Pentecost.

The Eucharist is given to us so that we too can encounter the risen Jesus – not face-to-face, chatting across the table, but in our uniting in worship with our fellow believers around the world and down through history. While we do not have Jesus' physical presence with us, as those Emmaus disciples did, we have his Holy Spirit to strengthen and inspire us to go out and share the good news of salvation with our hungry world.

What might have happened had those two disciples not urged Jesus to stay? Do we risk missing an encounter with God because we are not looking and listening for it?

Naomi Starkey

Don't just look – touch!

Luke 24:36b–39, 41–43

> Jesus himself stood among [the disciples] and said to them, 'Peace be with you.' They were startled and frightened, thinking they saw a ghost. He said to them, 'Why are you troubled, and why do doubts rise in your minds? Look at my hands and my feet. It is I myself! Touch me and see; a ghost does not have flesh and bones, as you see I have'... And while they still did not believe it because of joy and amazement, he asked them, 'Do you have anything here to eat?' They gave him a piece of broiled fish, and he took it and ate it in their presence. (NIV)

Reflection

Throughout these post-resurrection encounters, Jesus is preparing his followers for their work of going out and sharing the good news. It is consoling to see in this episode how he urges them to overcome their doubts and connect with him physically – look at him, touch him, watch him eat fish. He is no ghost, nor simply resuscitated, but made gloriously alive, while still scarred by his suffering. Even when the disciples' fear and doubt have turned to 'joy and amazement', they continue to struggle to grasp what is happening – and who is standing before them.

This episode is a counterbalance to Thomas' experience (John 20:24–29), when Jesus comments, 'Blessed are those who have not seen and yet have believed.' We can be tempted to hear that as 'Pathetic are those who lack really strong faith', but here we see there's no shame in wanting some kind of physical reassurance to build up our hesitant faith.

'Growing in faith' is sometimes felt to be a matter of simply cultivating a strong inner certainty – but the Eucharist provides a vital reminder that faith is also about seeing, touching, tasting and receiving what God wants to give us, literally as well as spiritually. Faith is also about living out what we believe in acts of witness to an indifferent world – caring for the needy, the lonely, the marginalised. We believe in an incarnate God; we need to model an incarnate faith too.

> In what ways could your church do more to model incarnate faith to the surrounding community?

Naomi Starkey

The Lord is here

John 6:8–13 (abridged)

Andrew, Simon Peter's brother, spoke up, 'Here is a boy with five small barley loaves and two small fish, but how far will they go among so many?' Jesus said, 'Make the people sit down'... Jesus then took the loaves, gave thanks, and distributed to those who were seated as much as they wanted. He did the same with the fish. When they had all had enough to eat, he said to the disciples, 'Gather the pieces that are left over. Let nothing be wasted.' So they gathered them and filled twelve baskets with the pieces of the five barley loaves left over. (NIV)

| Naomi Starkey

Reflection

This is the only miracle to feature in all four gospels, but only John uses the Greek word that gives us 'Eucharist' (Jesus 'gave thanks'), where the other gospels speak of him 'blessing' the bread. Interestingly, in John's version of the last supper, we do not hear of Jesus instituting this sacrament. Perhaps this version of miraculous feeding on the 'far shore of the Sea of Galilee' (v. 1) is John's way of exploring the matter.

What this passage shows us is Jesus accepting the meagre offering of a boy, probably from a poor background (barley loaves being much cheaper than wheat). Despite the lowly foodstuff, it becomes, through the grace and power of God, enough to feed a huge crowd – and enough to leave twelve baskets over (quite likely a symbolic number). The smallest of intentions are caught up and transformed by divine generosity.

For me, the Eucharist is the point at which worship intersects most directly with the kingdom of heaven, regardless of how we prefer to interpret what exactly happens during the prayer of consecration. In our worship, we listen to scripture expounded, we sing God's praises, we intercede for the world's needs, but it is in the Eucharist that we move most decisively from talking about and talking to God to receiving from him. God comes to us in bread and wine no matter how feeble our faith, how dark our doubts, how miserable our fears. We simply need to hold out our hands – no more than that.

> When the Lord is here, the very humblest gathering is hallowed.

| Liz Kent

Bread of heaven

John 6:32–35

> Jesus said to them, 'Very truly I tell you, it is not Moses who has given you the bread from heaven, but it is my Father who gives you the true bread from heaven. For the bread of God is the bread that comes down from heaven and gives life to the world.' 'Sir,' they said, 'always give us this bread.' Then Jesus declared, 'I am the bread of life. Whoever comes to me will never go hungry, and whoever believes in me will never be thirsty.'
>
> (NIV)

Reflection

At the beginning of John 6, Jesus feeds over 5,000 people with bread and fish. It is an encounter which causes the disciples to remember the history of the people of Israel on their way from slavery in Egypt, through the wilderness, to the promised land. Jesus' hearers had grown up understanding themselves as part of a chosen people whom God had miraculously fed with manna in the wilderness. Now, they had been part of a huge gathering of people on a mountainside, a 'wilderness place' far from the market where bread could be bought, and Jesus had taken two loaves of bread, blessed them and broken them to feed thousands of people.

Jesus directs their attention beyond physical food, and even beyond miraculously provided food, to the one who provides it: 'It is my Father who gives you the true bread from heaven.' In making this statement, Jesus links back to God's provision for Moses but takes them beyond that to consider Jesus as the one who has come from God the Father. While the disciples are still thinking about actual bread, Jesus makes the astonishing claim that *he* is the bread of life, the only one who can satisfy their deepest hunger.

Often we seek to satisfy the deepest hunger within us (maybe for affirmation, love, security, meaning or significance) by focusing on superficial snacks (likes on social media, possessions, achievements). In what area of your life might Jesus be directing you to come to him and let him meet that deep hunger?

> Lord Jesus, bread of life, fill me with yourself so I will not hunger for the things of this passing world. Amen

| Liz Kent

Jesus, the living bread

John 6:49–54

'Your ancestors ate the manna in the wilderness, yet they died. But here is the bread that comes down from heaven, which anyone may eat and not die. I am the living bread that came down from heaven. Whoever eats this bread will live forever. This bread is my flesh, which I will give for the life of the world.' Then the Jews began to argue sharply among themselves, 'How can this man give us his flesh to eat?' Jesus said to them, 'Very truly I tell you, unless you eat the flesh of the Son of Man and drink his blood, you have no life in you. Whoever eats my flesh and drinks my blood has eternal life, and I will raise them up at the last day.' (NIV)

| Liz Kent

Reflection

As the discussion in John 6 around manna and bread continues, the debate takes a turn, moving from 'bread which gives life' to 'living bread'. Jesus draws the parallel between the manna, which came from heaven, and himself as one alive and present with them, who has come from the Father in heaven. Jesus notes that even the celebrated heavenly manna only sustained the physical bodies of those who ate it. He broadens his hearer's vision from looking at what sustains them in this life to what endures for eternity. He points to himself as the one in whom eternal life can be found.

For those of us who have been shaped by the practice of sharing bread and wine in Communion (or the Eucharist – see the introduction, page 11), there is a familiarity to Jesus' words, but this call to eat Christ's flesh and drink his blood is shocking and confusing to those listening. The idea of eating Jesus' flesh and drinking his blood may also sound strange to contemporary ears, but in a culture which is increasingly defined by what we eat and drink, are there opportunities to explain this practice of 'participation in Christ'? What does it mean to 'feed on Jesus the living bread', taking his word and his Spirit into our lives?

> Eternal God, help me to know today that you are the living bread who gives life beyond the life I see before me. Amen

| Liz Kent

'Come and have breakfast'

John 21:8–13

The other disciples followed in the boat, towing the net full of fish, for they were not far from shore, about a hundred metres. When they landed, they saw a fire of burning coals there with fish on it, and some bread. Jesus said to them, 'Bring some of the fish you have just caught.' So Simon Peter climbed back into the boat and dragged the net ashore. It was full of large fish, 153, but even with so many the net was not torn. Jesus said to them, 'Come and have breakfast.' None of the disciples dared ask him, 'Who are you?' They knew it was the Lord. Jesus came, took the bread and gave it to them, and did the same with the fish.

(NIV)

| Liz Kent

Reflection

In this encounter, the risen Jesus goes to his disciples, who have returned to fishing after his death. On the beach, Jesus prepares breakfast and invites them to bring their own contribution of the fish they've just caught.

What is happening is astonishing. Only a little time before, Jesus had been crucified, and yet here he is, alive and present with them. At the same time, there is a sense of normality – fishing was what the disciples had done their whole lives. Bread and fish for breakfast was pretty normal, too. When Jesus takes the bread and gives it to them, they experience the resurrected Jesus present with them in the normality of a working day and an ordinary meal.

In the work canteen, Sarah always felt anxious and out of place. It was only when her colleague Jenny called to her 'come and have lunch with us' and offered her a seat at a table with two other colleagues that the fear began to subside. In the middle of an ordinary day, an extraordinary moment of invitation opened up a conversation over lunch which would change her life.

Where do you sense the presence of the risen Jesus in the ordinary meals you share with colleagues, friends or family?

> God of the extraordinary and the everyday, help me to remember as I break bread and eat 'ordinary' meals that you are present with me. As you invite me, help me invite others to meet you and encounter your love. Amen

Breaking bread in awe and thanksgiving

Acts 20:7–11a

On the first day of the week we came together to break bread. Paul spoke to the people and, because he intended to leave the next day, kept on talking until midnight. There were many lamps in the upstairs room where we were meeting. Seated in a window was a young man named Eutychus, who was sinking into a deep sleep as Paul talked on and on. When he was sound asleep, he fell to the ground from the third storey and was picked up dead. Paul went down, threw himself on the young man and put his arms around him. 'Don't be alarmed,' he said. 'He's alive!' Then he went upstairs again and broke bread and ate.

(NIV)

| Liz Kent

Reflection

The Christian community at Troas had come 'together to break bread' and the passage suggests this was their regular practice on 'the first day of the week'. Paul is visiting to teach and encourage the fledgling church, and he talks late into the night before the dramatic incident with Eutychus occurs.

The church had gathered with the intention of breaking bread to remember Jesus, but following the miraculous raising of Eutychus, their meeting has a fresh reason to give thanks to God. What began as the expected pattern (gathering to break bread), is disrupted by events (Eutychus' fall), but the outcome is a cause for thanksgiving ('He's alive!'), and the response is to break bread.

Have you ever gone to a church gathering, perhaps through habit or duty, and discovered God present and active in a way which surprised you? John Wesley, founder of Methodism, describes going 'unwillingly' to a Christian gathering in Aldersgate Street. There he experienced God's grace and assurance of forgiveness in an encounter which transformed his life. As we break bread to celebrate the risen Christ, we also give thanks for the change he has made in the lives of those who gather to worship him.

> Loving God, thank you for those times when we come to break bread and are filled with joy, wonder and gratitude for all you have done. Help me be open to seeing you work in unexpected ways and rejoice in your power to bring new life out of death. Amen

| Liz Kent

Breaking bread when everything is broken

Acts 27:33–38

Just before dawn Paul urged them all to eat. 'For the last fourteen days,' he said, 'you have been in constant suspense and have gone without food – you haven't eaten anything. Now I urge you to take some food. You need it to survive. Not one of you will lose a single hair from his head.' After he said this, he took some bread and gave thanks to God in front of them all. Then he broke it and began to eat. They were all encouraged and ate some food themselves. Altogether there were 276 of us on board. When they had eaten as much as they wanted, they lightened the ship by throwing the grain into the sea.

(NIV)

Reflection

Paul is being taken, under guard, to stand trial in Rome. Along with the guards and other prisoners, he is caught in a terrible storm. Paul's shipmates fear that they will not survive the voyage, and having thrown the cargo and ship's tackle overboard, they give up hope of rescue.

How strange it must have been for them that in the midst of fear and despair, Paul tells them they will come to no harm, urges them to eat, takes bread, gives thanks, breaks it and eats. In the face of imminent destruction, it seems to make no sense to do this, but perhaps this is where it makes the greatest sense.

It is in the times of greatest hardship, fear and despair that breaking bread becomes a symbolic act of trusting in God despite the external circumstances. It is here we remember that Christ, whose body was broken like the bread, overcame sin and death. To break bread in the midst of suffering and struggle causes us to remember Jesus, present with us in our situation, and not lose hope.

> God of compassion, thank you for all who witness to you in the face of suffering. Paul gave thanks, broke bread and remembered you during uncertain and dangerous times. Give us courage to share food and hope with others even when we are in the middle of difficult circumstances. Amen

Liz Kent

Small things with big consequences

1 Corinthians 5:6–8

Your boasting is not good. Don't you know that a little yeast leavens the whole batch of dough? Get rid of the old yeast, so that you may be a new unleavened batch – as you really are. For Christ, our Passover lamb, has been sacrificed. Therefore let us keep the Festival, not with the old bread leavened with malice and wickedness, but with the unleavened bread of sincerity and truth.

(NIV)

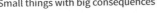

| Liz Kent

Reflection

In the Passover meal, unleavened bread is eaten. It is a reminder that there wasn't time for bread to rise when Moses and the Israelites fled Egypt. Before the Passover celebration, the house is cleaned to remove any trace of yeast or leavened bread. This is the picture Paul is painting for the Corinthian church: they are supposed to be living new life in Christ – the old ways and sinfulness have been swept out and they should be living as those who belong to Christ.

Unfortunately, some of the 'old yeast' has found its way into the community, and Paul uses bread imagery as a way of holding up a mirror to the church at Corinth. They would know how only a small amount of yeast can make a huge difference to the flour and water used to make bread. Paul points to the 'malice and wickedness' which is poisoning the fellowship and tells the Corinthians to get rid of it, as they would get rid of yeast before Passover.

The first time I made bread, I hadn't anticipated quite how dramatic an effect the yeast would have. I underestimated how large the loaf would become as my small portion of dough ballooned into a mound of bread which filled the oven! In the same way, I have seen how a small whisper of malicious gossip can expand to ruin a person's life, ministry or reputation and the fellowship of an entire church. Paul's wise counsel is to live as people of sincerity and truth and have nothing to do with the old ways of malice and wickedness.

> Lord of truth, cleanse my heart from all that would destroy your grace at work in my life and my community. Amen

Liz Kent

Connected and committed

1 Corinthians 10:16–21

Is not the cup of thanksgiving for which we give thanks a participation in the blood of Christ? And is not the bread that we break a participation in the body of Christ? Because there is one loaf, we, who are many, are one body, for we all share the one loaf. Consider the people of Israel: do not those who eat the sacrifices participate in the altar? Do I mean then that food sacrificed to an idol is anything, or that an idol is anything? No, but the sacrifices of pagans are offered to demons, not to God, and I do not want you to be participants with demons. You cannot drink the cup of the Lord and the cup of demons too; you cannot have a part in both the Lord's table and the table of demons.

(NIV)

| Liz Kent

Reflection

'You are what you eat', according to the slogan, and in this passage Paul takes this further by linking eating and participating. Paul notes that to eat in a religious setting is a means of participating in that religion.

The Christians in Corinth came from both Jewish and Gentile backgrounds, so Paul chooses religious examples from both contexts to make his point. For Jewish hearers, he gives the example of eating the meat of sacrifices. For Gentile hearers, he refers to the pagan rituals. His point is that in eating and drinking we are joined with those who eat and drink the same things with us. Corinthians who followed Jesus had to leave behind their old practice of feasting at the worship places of pagan gods. To eat both there and at the Lord's table was an attempt to participate in two incompatible ways of life.

Sharing in the one loaf connected Christians to Christ and to one another and required a level of commitment which excluded giving worship or loyalty to any other so-called deity. Sometimes we have to make tough choices about what we will participate in if it threatens to compromise our relationship with Christ.

> Lord Jesus, when I am tempted to compromise my commitment to you, remind me that I belong to you, as part of your body, and give me courage to follow you alone.
> Amen

Liz Kent

Eat, drink, remember

1 Corinthians 11:23–26

For I received from the Lord what I also passed on to you: the Lord Jesus, on the night he was betrayed, took bread, and when he had given thanks, he broke it and said, 'This is my body, which is for you; do this in remembrance of me.' In the same way, after supper he took the cup, saying, 'This cup is the new covenant in my blood; do this, whenever you drink it, in remembrance of me.' For whenever you eat this bread and drink this cup, you proclaim the Lord's death until he comes. (NIV)

| Liz Kent

Reflection

This passage contains what has come to be recognised as the most succinct description of the practice of Communion in the early church.

Paul is clear with the Corinthians that what he is transmitting to them is the practice which he received. It contains the actions of thanksgiving, breaking bread, drinking wine and remembering. Together, these practices witness to what has taken place in Jesus' death and also look to the future hope of his promised return.

The emphasis on 'in remembrance' means that Communion liturgies are focused around retelling the story of God's saving love made visible in the life, death and resurrection of Jesus. In eating bread and drinking wine, we remember Jesus with thanksgiving. The beautiful simplicity of the act of breaking bread and sharing wine means it crosses language, national and cultural boundaries. Christians across the world may differ in many ways, but in the central act of sharing bread and wine we are drawn to the heart of our faith: remembering Jesus.

Micah grew up in Uganda but came to study in the UK. He had been involved in his church at home and searched for a church near his student flat. He went one Sunday and found the songs were different, the preaching style was unfamiliar to him, the people were friendly but reserved, the church notices were nothing like at home. It was only as the bread was broken, the wine poured and both were shared that he felt he was truly part of the body of Christ.

> Lord Jesus, thank you that through the mystery,
> you come to us in the simplicity of bread and wine.
> Help me remember you today. Amen

Liz Kent

Discerning the body

1 Corinthians 11:27–29, 33–34a

So then, whoever eats the bread or drinks the cup of the Lord in an unworthy manner will be guilty of sinning against the body and blood of the Lord. Everyone ought to examine themselves before they eat of the bread and drink from the cup. For those who eat and drink without discerning the body of Christ eat and drink judgment on themselves... So then, my brothers and sisters, when you gather to eat, you should all eat together. Anyone who is hungry should eat something at home, so that when you meet together it may not result in judgment. (NIV)

Reflection

The church at Corinth contained believers from different social backgrounds, with rich and poor breaking bread together. Unfortunately, a meal which was supposed to centre around the self-giving love of God in Jesus had become a selfish free-for-all. In his letter to them, Paul draws the church back to the purpose of their gathering, to eat together, discerning that the risen Christ is present among them.

To discern the body of Christ requires Christians to be aware of the needs of others within that body. To selfishly eat the meal, only caring about oneself, flies in the face of Jesus' command to love one another in his new community. This passage reminds us that it is often within the context of breaking bread that we become aware that we need to confess our sin. It also reminds us of the need to be mindful of our brothers and sisters.

As Katie read this passage, she thought about the images she'd seen in the news of famine in South Sudan and wondered how the Christians living there were surviving. Should she even take Communion if her brothers and sisters in Christ were starving? As she prayed and struggled to find an answer, she felt she should respond by fasting one day a week and giving the money she would have spent on food to a food relief programme working in South Sudan. It was one small action, but it was an act of solidarity, seeking to discern the body of Christ.

> When we have ignored you by ignoring one of your children – Lord, forgive us. When we have eaten our fill and left others to go hungry – Lord, forgive us. When we have broken bread and neglected the broken – Lord, forgive us.
> Amen

| Liz Kent

Eating and acceptance

Revelation 3:20–22

'Here I am! I stand at the door and knock. If anyone hears my voice and opens the door, I will come in and eat with that person, and they with me. To the one who is victorious, I will give the right to sit with me on my throne, just as I was victorious and sat down with my Father on his throne. Whoever has ears, let them hear what the Spirit says to the churches.'

(NIV)

| Liz Kent

Reflection

In many cultures, to eat with someone is the ultimate sign of acceptance. If hospitality is extended, you are welcomed as a friend. To refuse to eat with someone in many places is to dishonour them. This notion of eating as acceptance is why Jesus got in such trouble with the Pharisees for eating with 'tax collectors and sinners'. To eat with them was seen as an affirmation of who they were and what they did or what they stood for.

Gathering over a meal is often a way of deepening a relationship or nurturing a friendship. When John signed up to the Alpha Course, he was surprised that the first part of the evening involved sharing a meal. As the weeks went by, people he'd met as strangers became friends, as food and stories and opinions were shared across the table. He found the companionship he'd been seeking but was also becoming aware that Jesus was knocking on the door of his heart.

> The word 'companion' comes from the words for 'with' and 'bread' – a companion is literally 'one whom I eat bread with'. The invitation of Jesus in Revelation 3:20 to companionship in his kingdom is the ultimate invitation to friendship with God for eternity.

Whole-church resources

Individual copy £4.99

Holy Habits is an adventure in Christian discipleship. Inspired by Luke's model of church found in Acts 2:42–47, it identifies ten habits and encourages the development of a way of life formed by them. These resources are designed to help churches explore the habits creatively in a range of contexts and live them out in whole-life, intergenerational, missional discipleship.

MISSIONAL DISCIPLESHIP RESOURCES FOR CHURCHES

HOLY**HABITS**

These new additions to the Holy Habits resources have been developed to help churches and individuals explore the Holy Habits through prayerful engagement with the Bible and live them out in whole-life, missional discipleship.

Bible Reflections   Edited by Andrew Roberts | Individual copy £3.99

Each set of Bible reading notes contains eight weeks of devotional material. Four writers bring different perspectives on the habit in question through their reflections on passages drawn from across the Bible narrative.

Group Studies   Edited by Andrew Roberts | Individual copy £6.99

Each leader's guide contains eight sessions of Bible study material, providing off-the-peg material to help churches get started or continue with Holy Habits. Each session includes a Bible passage, reflections, group questions, community/outreach ideas, art and media links and a prayer.

Find out more at holyhabits.org.uk
and brfonline.org.uk/collections/holy-habits
Download a leaflet for your church leadership at
brfonline.org.uk/holyhabitsdownload

Are you looking to continue the habit of daily Bible reading?

With a subscription to BRF Bible reading notes, you'll have everything you need to nourish your relationship with the Bible and with God.

Our most popular and longest running series, *New Daylight*, features daily readings and reflections from a selection of much-beloved writers, dealing with a variety of themes and Bible passages. With the relevant passage printed alongside the comment, *New Daylight* is a practical and effective way of reading the Bible as a part of your everyday routine.

New Daylight is available in print, deluxe (large print), by email and as an app for iOS and Android.

'I think Bible reading notes are really underrated. At any age – there I was as a teenager getting as much out of them then as I am now – so they're for every age group, not just the very young and the very old. I think to have them as your bedside companion is a really wise idea throughout life.'
Debbie Thrower, Pioneer of BRF's Anna Chaplaincy programme

JANUARY–APRIL 2020

New Daylight

Sustaining your daily journey with the Bible

Included in this issue
Genesis 37–45: Joseph AMANDA BLOOR
What hath God wrought! MURDO MACDONALD
Gardens in the Bible BARBARA MOSSE

Also available:

Find out more at brfonline.org.uk

Praise for the original Holy Habits resources

'Here are some varied and rich resources to help further deepen our discipleship of Christ, encouraging and enabling us to adopt the life-transforming habits that make for following Jesus.'
Revd Dr Martyn Atkins, Team Leader & Superintendent Minister, Methodist Central Hall, Westminster

'The Holy Habits resources will help you, your church, your fellowship group, to engage in a journey of discovery about what it really means to be a disciple today. I know you will be encouraged, challenged and inspired as you read and work your way through… There is lots to study together and pray about, and that can only be good as our churches today seek to bring about the kingdom of God.'
Revd Loraine Mellor, President of the Methodist Conference 2017/18

'The Holy Habits resources help weave the spiritual through everyday life. They're a great tool that just get better with use. They help us grow in our desire to follow Jesus as their concern is formation not simply information.'
Olive Fleming Drane and John Drane

'The Holy Habits resources are an insightful and comprehensive manual for living in the way of Jesus in the 21st century: an imaginative, faithful and practical gift for the church that will sustain and invigorate our life and mission in a demanding world. The Holy Habits resources are potentially transformational for a church.'
Revd Ian Adams, Mission Spirituality Adviser for Church Mission Society

'To understand the disciplines of the Christian life without practising them habitually is like owning a fine collection of soap but never having a wash. The team behind Holy Habits knows this, which is why they have produced these excellent and practical resources. Use them, and by God's grace you will grow in holiness.'
Paul Bayes, Bishop of Liverpool